New York
from the air

vmb
PUBLISHERS

New York
from the air

1 The pyramidal roof of 40 Wall Street reflects a bygone age of elegant design and detail.

2-3 Extensively restored, with its gold-leafed torch ablaze at night, the Statue of Liberty salutes an American ideal of liberty.

4-5 Historic Battery Park, with its circular Ft. Clinton, dominates Manhattan's southern tip. Here the Hudson River and the East River flow into Upper New York Harbor. On the left rises Battery Park City; to the right the Financial District and Wall Street.

6-7 Central Park, the city's jewel, extends from 59th to 110th Street. Flanking the park are the luxury apartment houses of Central Park West (left) and Fifth Avenue (right), with the Metropolitan Museum just below Jacqueline Kennedy Onassis Reservoir.

8 The Hudson River is flanked by Battery Park City and (right) by older office buildings. The 'beehive' building (bottom left) is the Holocaust Museum.

9 The Empire State Building, at the crossing of Fifth Avenue and 34th Street is the heart of Mid-Manhattan.

vmb

VMB Publishers®
An imprint of White Star, Italy

© 2005 White Star S.p.A.
Via Candido Sassone, 22/24 - 13100 Vercelli, Italy
www.whitestar.it

ISBN 88-540-0209-7

Reprints:
1 2 3 4 5 6   09 08 07 06 05

Printed in Thailand
Color separation by Chiaroscuro, Turin

Photographs Antonio Attini

Text Peter Skinner

Graphic Design Marinella Debernardi

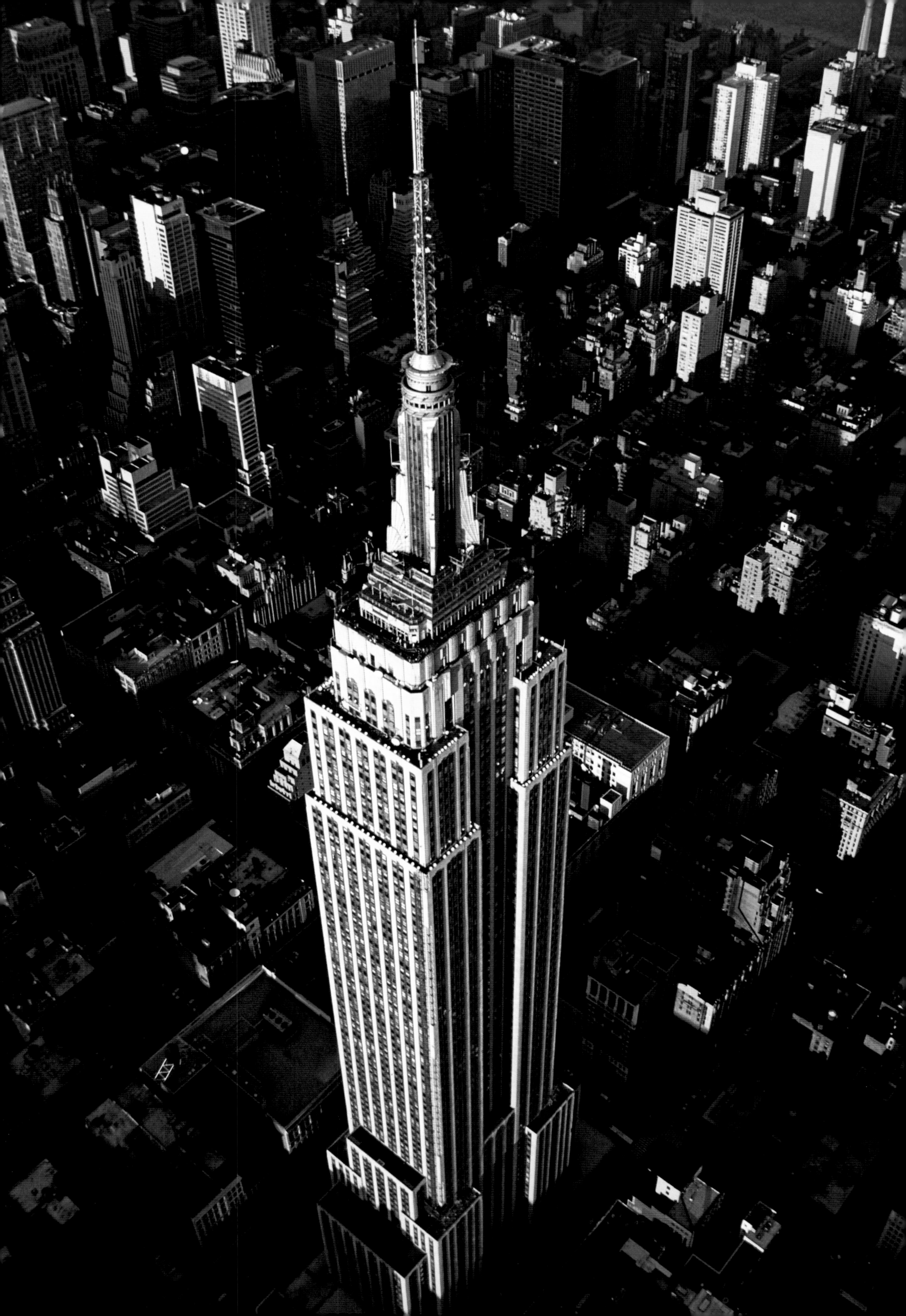

Introduction

"New York," like other world-cities, defies easy description; it is too diverse and contains too much. For every public image – Wall Street brokers in their office towers, nerve-wracking traffic, crowd-mobbed celebrities, etc. – there's a countervailing private image – the artist in a waterside studio, the solitary stroller in wooded parkland, the serene Chinese calligraphy teacher, etc. Many visitors arriving in New York eager to map their own impressions find that they can't easily get to grips with the city: Just what, they ask, is 'New York'?

Anyone getting a panoramic view of New York City from the air (and quite a few airborne arrivals do) would be looking down on five areas – four of them densely settled. The long, slender island of Manhattan would be instantly recognizable. The massy fingerprint of Staten Island, twice Manhattan's size, would be recognizable. But there's also Brooklyn, Queens and the Bronx, all parts of New York City, all three separated from Manhattan by rivers but variously linked by bridges and tunnels. All in all, the geography of New York City poses problems for the visitor: just where does Brooklyn become Queens? And where is Queens' farther boundary – and what comes next? It's easy to see where the Bronx begins, across the narrow river at Manhattan's northern tip, but just where does it end? And why is Manhattan so often called "New York" if there's so much more that is New York?

A map will help with the city-as-parts and the city-as-a-whole problem, but will not explain governance issues. Each of the five named areas is a borough of New York City but also a county of New York State. Manhattan is New York County; Brooklyn is Kings County; the Bronx is Bronx County, Queens is Queens County; and Staten Island is Richmond County.

So exactly what's meant by "New York"? Though it should mean the whole city, for many residents New York usually means only Manhattan. And that's not all: people in the outer boroughs (particularly in Staten Island) often call Manhattan "the city" . . . and many maps name the Hudson the North River . . .

Today's five-borough New York is a young city; the act of consolidation that created it was passed hardly a century ago, in 1898 – opposed by a fiercely independent Brooklyn. Though in many ways an ultra-modern city, New York – all five boroughs – are proud of their local histories. They differ markedly in one respect, which can be basically stated thus: whereas Manhattan's first southern-tip settlement rolled determinedly north up the 2 mile by 12 mile island (swallowing up a few small villages en route), in all the other boroughs, separate little settlements slowly expanded and finally coalesced into borough-wide urban areas. Actual patterns differed; historically, Brooklyn, for example, maintained an industrial base while Queens was more residential.

More than in any other world-city, New York's growth has been driven by immigration; around the turn of the century each year a million or so immigrants entered the United States via New York. Mercifully, by no means all stayed within the city. But so many did that whole areas of new housing sprang up, particularly along the fast-expanding subway routes, with schools, churches and institutional buildings following. The miracle of New York is its diversity: the boroughs retain strong identities. Each has its own rich array of educational, cultural and recreational facilities, but textures often differ; street layouts, housing, churches, colleges, institutional buildings, parks, and residents reflect different ethnic backgrounds, and result in vibrant and exciting neighborhoods.

Anyone seeing New York from the air in any sort of leisurely circuit would be struck by the fact that Manhattan is the smallest borough. They would also be struck by how much parkland each borough has, quite often at the shore. Of course, the various sections and neighborhoods of each borough are not equally well served, though the creation of miniparks has somewhat improved the situation. Aerial photography over major cities is a challenging business. Security and safety regulations often preclude specific desirable shots and thus the bigger more easily visible sites and features are photographed more often than smaller, more 'hidden' ones. Each of New York's five boroughs has at least one surviving 18th-century house, but not all are freestanding in open setting; they get lost in the mosaic.

The pattern of settlement in New York is not easy to capture as many earlier communities with their farms, mills and churches were simply torn down when the land was bought up for redevelopment. Increasingly the old ethnic enclaves and neighborhoods have become mixed. Time was when Italians, Irish, Scandinavians (particularly Norwegians), Germans, Poles, Czechs, Hungarians, Ukrainians, Chinese, Jews and others lived in quite clearly defined neighborhoods, both in Manhattan and often in the other boroughs, with their own churches, breweries, food stores, newspapers and associations. After World War II, greater

11 A satellite view of the lower tip of Manhattan.

12 This satellite view shows Central Park and East and Upper West Sides.

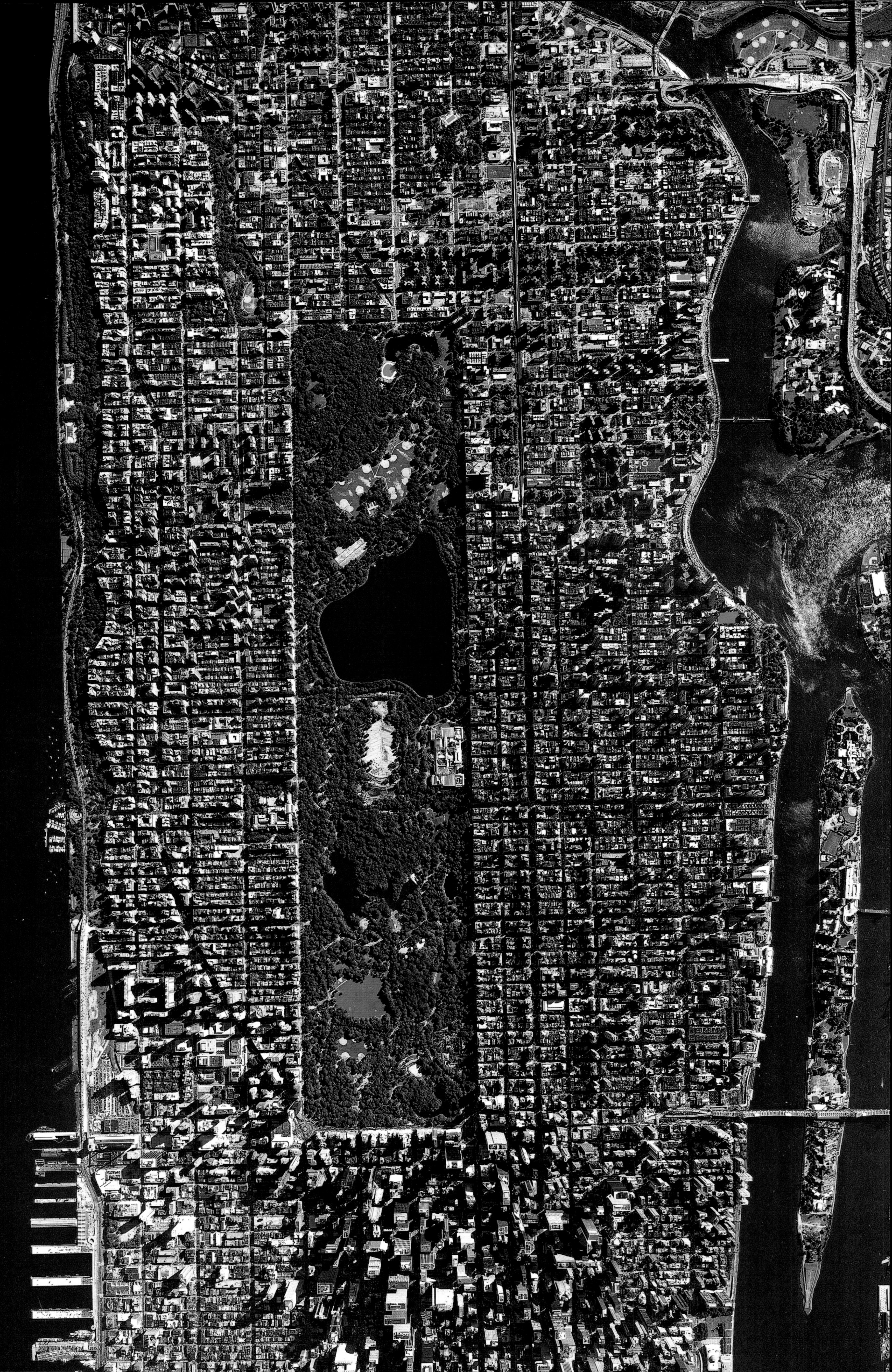

social mobility and the rapid development of Long Island, where new townships sprang up in the potato fields, led to the slow but progressive dilution of most of these ethnic neighborhoods. However, though the German and Hungarian communities may be only a shadow of their previous selves, Chinatown and Little Italy remain vibrant – much helped by being big attractions for visitors. Patches of the old Lower East Side, with its declining Jewish population survive, but largely as specific shopping streets.

Concurrently, new ethnic neighborhoods are developing, particularly in the boroughs. Woodside and Jackson Heights in Queens are remarkably mixed, but within the mix are concentrations of people from specific Latin-American and Caribbean nations, while Flushing is known for Indians from the subcontinent and for Koreans and other Asians. One or two blocks in Central Brooklyn are home to many members of New York's modest Tibetan population, while Bay Ridge, losing its Norwegians, has welcomed newcomers from a number of Muslim nations. Overall, new immigrants are not at all as clustered as those of a half-century ago; the ethnic tapestry has a richer and more varied pattern. Such is the new mix that a school class of 30 children may represent 20 or more nationalities. Some parents may be basically monolingual – and it is not unusual to see their children interpreting for them.

Certain callings attract specific ethnic groups. Many Albanians have become apartment house superintendents; Koreans operate numerous small 24-hour-per day neighborhood groceries; Pakistanis manage an immense number of newsstands; Afghanis are the deft chefs in hot chicken outlets, Uzbeks efficiently repair shoes, Mexican chefs prepare an amazing amount of non-Mexican food, to name but a few. And in almost every case these hardworking individuals are determined to ensure college educations and white-collar careers for their children.

New York's many ethnic groups add greatly to the city's cultural life. Not only is food and other shopping much more rewarding, but cultural festivals and events from Irish theater through Indian dance to Korean opera are a delight, to say nothing of proudly celebrated 'annual days' such as Puerto-Rican Day and numerous exuberant street fairs. Unless a series of pictures is taken over time, photography captures the scene of the moment rather than registering change. It's difficult to convey to any visitor the sheer rate of change – change for the better – that is occurring throughout New York. The mentality that led

to the destruction of Penn Station, deemed by many to have been an act of vandalism, and the threat of a similar fate for Grand Central Terminal, is much less evident. Many fine buildings no longer economically serving their original functions are converted to new uses; notably, the dowager office towers of Lower Manhattan are becoming residential. Similarly, Greek-temple style banks, deconsecrated disused churches, and unneeded fire stations have become housing or retail stores as appropriate.

The architectural design of public facilities has come under the spotlight. No longer will the economic, drab but functional structure suffice. In part, the plans for rebuilding the World Trade Center site have heightened aesthetic awareness. Notably, the Santiago Calatrava's stunning design for a major subway interchange station at the WTC breaks new ground, as does the design for the neighboring Fulton Street multi-line station, and plans for a new Amtrak terminal in the soon-to-be-relinquished General Post Office on 33rd St. and Eighth Avenue. Recreational facilities are also being upgraded. Central Park has been restored to pristine condition; the lessons learned are being applied to other parks in other boroughs, though funds, particularly private funds, are scarce. Citywide, citizens are finding a new voice – and, if need be, are willing to press their claims in court.

New York City is gaining recreation areas and parks through the continuing transformation of the waterfront into usable public space. Thousands of small irregular plots – even isolated within highway junctions – have been planted, fenced and lit. Increasingly, 'street furniture' – bus stop shelters, phone kiosks, newsstands, waste bins, bike racks and signage – are being upgraded. All these improvements are citywide, involving all five boroughs; they are subject to much discussion and many demands for further civic improvements. One factor has been the huge increase in Manhattan rents. As more and more young professional couples and singles move to areas of the outer boroughs once considered working class, they bring professional expectations and activist skills with them, creating attractive new communities.

This album captures some of Manhattan's historic sections, featuring both the old and the new. It also journeys farther afield, presenting an introductory glance at the immense stretch of Upper Manhattan, and visiting the outer boroughs and some of the city's far-flung waterfronts, a world apart, so different from the Manhattan's urban density.

14-15 Three historic skyscrapers anchor Mid-Manhattan: bottom left, the McGraw-Hill Building; and toward the East River and Queens rises the silver-spired Chrysler Building. To the right, the Empire State Building, with Brooklyn across the East River.

16-17 This spectacular view shows Brooklyn and Manhattan Bridge connecting Manhattan to Brooklyn.

18-19 Warm linght embraces the Empire State Building with its 86th-floor observation deck which draws over 3.5 million visitors annually.

LOWER MANHATTAN

"Lower Manhattan" has rolled north: past wall-less Wall Street; past canal-less Canal Street; past 14th St. and up to 23rd St. A blend of old and new streets and buildings, vibrant ethnic enclaves and distinctive neighborhoods, with water on three sides – the Bay, the East River and the Hudson – it's an exciting area

At the tip of Manhattan sits Battery Park (the city's oldest) and Castle Clinton – not a "castle" but a circular fort built on the Battery to protect Lower Manhattan. It demonstrates New York's genius for recycling buildings, having been a concert venue where Jenny Lind, "the Swedish Nightingale," sang and where General Tom Thumb was an exhibit. Then, before Ellis Island opened, the building became an immigration station; now it is a fully restored historic site.

In dramatic contrast, nearby Battery Park City is one of New York's newest planned communities. The rock excavated for the World Trade Center was dumped in the Hudson and forms the 20-block development's foundation layer. A broad tree-lined esplanade fronts the Hudson; inland, well-spaced apartment houses stand on green sites extending twenty bocks. At the midpoint are the three towers of the World Financial Center, topped respectively by a mastaba, a dome, and a stepped pyramid, green-tinted against the buff stone facing. In rear is the World Trade Center site. The twin towers' cleared "footprints" are reminders of the tragedy, but to the north of the site reconstruction of the 7 WTC office tower is a symbol of New York City's indomitable optimism.

Anyone walking through the canyons of the Wall Street area should slip into the lobbies of the grand old buildings. No empty rectangles of black marble, no stainless steel and fluorescent-light sterility; instead, handsome spaces with walls of colored marbles, coffered ceilings, chandeliers, and bronze fittings. The external masonry is rich in architectural detailing; the roof lines sport iconic pyramids or Gothic-trim mansards. From the Staten Island ferry, the old vs the new, the spire vs the flat top is seen to advantage. But the tide has turned: the International style is out; newer buildings are not ashamed of decorative features.

The South Street Seaport beckons to all who seek "Old" Manhattan. Here on the East River, rescued and restored vessels are docked against a backdrop of restored 19th-century ship chandlers' and merchants' premises. More than a living museum, the Seaport is a vibrant shopping and dining area, with tables dotting the cobblestoned slips where in times past men handled the cargoes from which much of the city's wealth derived.

Broadway, which follows an old Indian trail leading north, is always thronged with visitors, and the adjoining City Hall Park is an ideal place for a pause. Set amid the world's most expensive real estate, it is an oasis of calm against an eclectic backdrop of buildings: the Renaissance-style City Hall and the severely Neo-Classical Tweed Courthouse frame the park; just beyond loom the Municipal Building with its Baroque cupola and the Neo-Gothic Woolworth Building. These four icons reflect Lower Manhattan's visual richness and its role as the city's governmental and commercial heart.

Since the first Dutch settlement of 1624, New York has welcomed immigrants from almost every country of the world. Chinatown, with many immigrants arriving in the mid-1800s, remains a thriving community. Smaller, older buildings with shops below and accommodation above is the common pattern; Bayard, Pell, and neighboring streets are perfect examples.

Crossing Canal Street, to the northeast of Chinatown, leads the visitor into Little Italy, also proud of its colorfulness and traditions and drawing visitors to its many restaurants and cafés and to the religious festivals that mark the year. Mulberry and Grand Streets, in the heart of Little Italy, are thronged with visitors year round.

Bridges are one of Lower Manhattan's major visual highlights, the more so because their ramps begin well inland and rise above waterfront streets. Such was the challenge of building spans over the East River that the bridges offer proud, almost triumphal approaches. Leading off Canal Street is the colonnaded approach to the Manhattan Bridge (opened in 1909), the middle one of the three bridges that take Manhattanites to Brooklyn. Farther south is the Brooklyn Bridge (opened in 1889); farther north is the Williamsburg Bridge (opened 1903). All three have popular pedestrian walkways. The Brooklyn Bridge predated the earliest subway, but other two carry subway tracks in addition to their roadways. The bridges' long approach ramps, rising high above the streets, offer a wonderful range of views over and into buildings lying below.

Lower Manhattan is known for its bargain shopping. Flanking the East River is the Lower East Side, with the Delancey Street as its spine. It is no longer an entirely Jewish neighborhood; residents began to seek

20-21 from left to right
The office towers of
Lower Manhattan; the
Statue of Liberty; and
the Brooklyn and
Manhattan bridges.

23 The Woolworth
Building, once known
"the Cathedral of
Commerce," was
designed to bestow
dignity on commerce.

less crowded neighborhoods after World War II. Nonetheless, the area's synagogues, kosher butcher shops and restaurants, and its many small clothing stores, gift shops, and other retail establishments, with their wares spilling onto shop-front racks and sidewalk tables, reflect Jewish traditions in serving an increasingly mixed population – often Sunday shoppers from elsewhere in Manhattan or from the outer boroughs.

To the west of the Lower East Side, beyond Little Italy, lies Soho ("South of Houston" [St]), an area of old manufacturing lofts that are now generally avant-garde art and style galleries, high-fashion salons, and expensive restaurants, with multimillion-dollar 'loft' apartments on the upper floors. Joining the scramble for instant fashionability is self-created Tribeca ("Triangle above Canal [St.]," where a similar art-style-fashion-and-dining scene has taken root.

Houston St. (more or less 1st St.), a river-to-river thoroughfare, marks the beginning of two "villages" that continue north to 14th St., also a broad river-to-river thoroughfare. Greenwich Village (extending from Broadway to the Hudson) is a genuine village with 18th-century roots, a country escape for the Dutch and then the British settlers clustered around the Battery. Washington Square Park, host to open-air music and theater programs, with its smaller-scale "Arc de Triomphe" at the foot of Fifth Avenue, is the Village's central meeting place; around it are New York University buildings – whose student population keeps the Village youthful. A mix of handsome town houses, dignified older apartment buildings and turn-of-the century tenements on often charming tree-lined small streets, home to many specialty shops and renowned restaurants old and new, give the Village its special residential flavor.

Along the Hudson Greenwich Village (now called the West Village) is undergoing dramatic change. A continuous strip of waterfront park has been built, with access to restored piers, one sporting a café, seating, and an airy pavilion. Inland, new steel and glass highrises are being heavily criticized as destroying the historic ambience and character of the Village. Many gay couples and single gay men live in the area; their sense of style is reflected in the stores, cafés, and street life.

From Broadway to the East River another "Village" exists: the East Village, a real estate marketing invention. This area of tenement buildings that extends over to the East River is probably home to more one-of-kind stores within a single small area than anywhere else in New York. African art, Burmese restaurants, Tibetan antiques, Ukrainian books, acupuncture, aromatherapy supplies, brass furniture fittings, herbal remedies, macramé work, reflexology and theater, dance, music, and foreign films – the East Village offers them all. It is home to Polish and Ukrainian communities, to Hells Angels, rockers, punk and all else that can be imagined. The East Village draws many of New York's most talented young artists; with them come an army of artsy hopefuls.

The East Village boasts a number of distinguished buildings, among them the Cooper Union (opened as an engineering school in 1853 by Peter Cooper, a cast-iron pioneer). In 1860, President Lincoln gave a speech in the Union's Great Hall. Tompkins Square Park (site of short-lived communes, squatter settlements, and demonstrations) is the community's biggest park.

Lower Manhattan's northern section, from 14th to 23rd Sts, marks the start of "grid-plan New York." Gone are the tight clusters of sometimes curving or dog-leg streets found around the Battery and in Chinatown; gone is Greenwich Village's on-the-diagonal street plan. Here regularity is the hallmark, though the parallel the avenues and streets have much of interest. Union Square at 14th St. and Broadway, famed for protest rallies, is also the site of a Greenmarket selling local fresh farm produce, while the private Gramercy Park on 20th Street, a genteel oasis, erupts into lawsuits if a tree is trimmed. To the east, extending from First Avenue to the East River, are two almost self-contained communities: the immense multiblock housing developments of Stuyvesant Town and Peter Cooper Village, with their brick towers rising in orderly ranks from a green park base. Stuyvesant Square, a park bisected by Second Avenue, is a nearby quiet oasis.

"Big" is the fingerprint elsewhere too. Toward the Hudson, the brick monolith of the Port Authority Building occupies an entire block at 16th St.; north at 20th Street the red-brick Gothic-style buildings of the Union Theological Seminary, occupy another. Extending around a grassy courtyard it seems to be an Oxford or Cambridge college airlifted from Great Britain

At 23rd St, where Broadway (on the diagonal) crosses Fifth Avenue, stands the landmark Flatiron Building, built in 1902 and now named for its shape. New York's earliest true skyscraper, its predates the Woolworth Building, built in 1913. To the north are the massed tower of Mid-Manttan.

24 The multilane highway going north once flanked the Hudson River. Today it separates

Battery Park City (built on landfill in the 1970s) from neighboring Manhattan.

26-27 Battery Park City's Esplanade is a major amenity enhanced by trees, flower plantings and river breezes. Top

left is the 'Gothic' Woolworth building; center top is 40 Wall Street, with its distinctive green pyramid roof.

28 *Battery Park City's new apartment houses look onto the tree-lined Esplanade fronting the Hudson River.*

28-29 *The World Financial Center, with its towers topped by the green dome and truncated pyramid, is* the main entry to waterfront Battery Park City. Here one tower is ablaze with light.

29 top *North Cove is a yacht-fancier's paradise that offers Lower Manhattan residents a new recreation.*

30-31 *Two characteristics define downtown buildings: they conform to the old 17th-century curving streets, and* the old dowager skyscrapers are known for their decorative and intricately patterned architecture.

*32 top and 32-33
The Municipal
Building (left and
center foreground),
City Hall in its
wooded park, and
the soaring white
stone Woolworth
Building hark back*

*to an era of
gracious
architecture and
generous
ornamentation. The
ornate cupola of the
Municipal Building
is a much-loved
landmark.*

*32 bottom Infinite
gradation
characterizes the
summits of many
buildings dated the
first decades of last
century.*

34 top Classical architectural roof treatments in metallic blue are keynotes of the World Financial Center's towers.

34 bottom The narrowing of Lower Manhattan is clearly shown here: top left are the Brooklyn and Manhattan bridges, spanning the East River.

35 The World Financial Center, North Cove and the Hudson offer residents urban life with nature at hand.

36 top Lower Manhattan's clustered towers nod to Brooklyn's piers. Many people working in Lower Manhattan live across the river in conveniently close Brooklyn.

36-37 The Brooklyn and Manhattan bridges link downtown

Brooklyn to Manhattan. The tree-lined Brooklyn Heights Esplanade (above the twin piers) provides a great view of Lower Manhattan.

37 Though appearing delicate, the Manhattan Bridge carries road, rail, and pedestrian traffic.

38-39 The Brooklyn Bridge, the Manhattan Bridge and, far right, the Williamsburg Bridge, all span the East River. Brooklyn is at the base of the photograph.

40-41 In good weather the center walkway across the Brooklyn Bridge is thronged with pedestrians.

42 top The Williamsburg Bridge (left) and the Brooklyn Bridge (right) demonstrate the intricate ties and strengtheners of early bridges.

42-43 The restored South Street Seaport lies just south of the Brooklyn Bridge; the slender white spire of the Woolworth Building marks Lower Broadway.

43 The Williamsburg Bridge, north of the Broooklyn and Manhattan bridges, completes the trio of downtown East River spans.

44-45 The Brooklyn waterfront below the Manhattan and Brooklyn bridges has been redeveloped into attractive miniparks.

46-47 *The designers of the Manhattan Bridge, completed in 1909, chose steel over stone for the bridge towers and adopted numerous decorative elements to differentiate their bridge from the Brooklyn Bridge, completed in 1883.*

48-49 The South
Street Seaport
represents history
preserved: center
and right on the
mainland are
restored 19th-
century buildings.

49 top The
afterdeck of a 19th-
century sailing
vessel. The South
Street Seaport's
"saved" vessels have
been, or are being,
expertly restored.

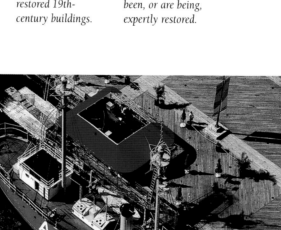

49 center Before
honorable retirement
is 1967, the Ambrose
Light Ship was
stationed in Lower
New York Bay. The
light tower that
replaced it was hit by
a ship in 1996, and
had to be replaced by
a second one.

49 bottom The
Seaport's waterfront,
with its many
restaurants, bars,
and stores, is a
popular warm-
weather rendezvous
for New Yorkers and
visitors alike.

50 The masonry-
clad, copper-roofed
cupola-topped
building at 40 Wall
Street proudly
displays
architectural trim
too expensive for
cut-price modernity.

51 top left The
elegant three-story
City Hall,
combining French
Renaissance and
Georgian styles,
with its delicate
cupola, is a happy
survival from 1811.

51 top right The
flat roofs of modern
office towers
support an amazing
variety of
mechanical
equipment, invisible
from below.

51 bottom The
magnificent
colonnaded
approach to the

Manhattan Bridge
has been
restored to its
former glory.

52-53 The spires of
the 70 Pine Street
and 40 Wall Street
frame the tree-lined
Brooklyn Heights
Esplanade, behind
which rise 19th-
century houses.

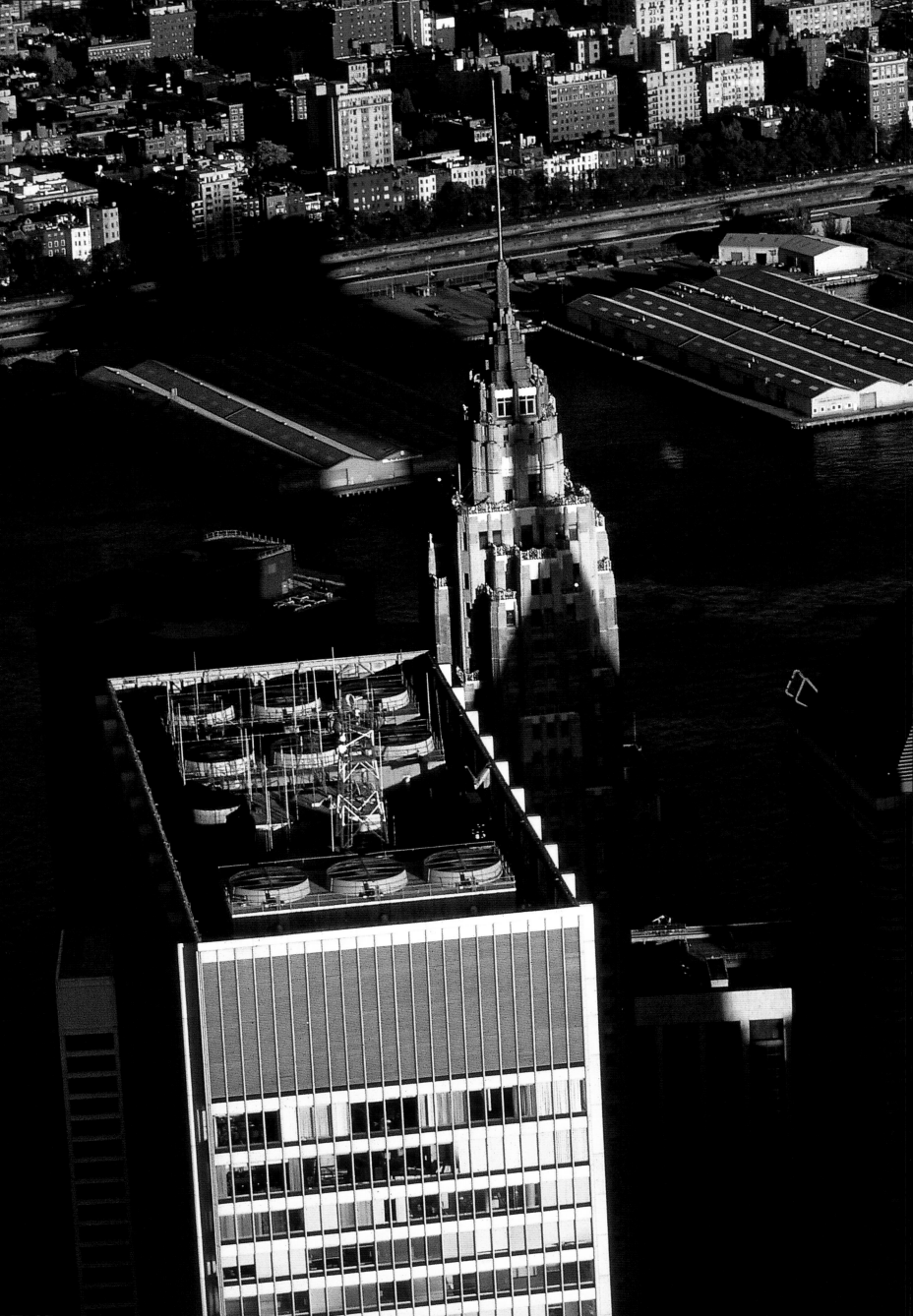

54 19th- and 20th-century buildings, both high-rise and low-rise, pack the narrow streets of Lower Manhattan, where older office buildings are becoming residential.

55 Lower Manhattan boasts much distinctive architecture: to the left, the curved-façade new Federal Building, to its right the pyramid-capped Federal Courthouse; close by the cupola's Municipal Building, and front right, the Woolworth Building with its 'Gothic' ornamentation.

56-57 The Williamsburg Bridge connects Manhattan and Brooklyn (top); below the four-chimneyed generating plant is the huge Stuyvesant Town-Peter Cooper Village housing development.

58-59 The headquarters of Con Edison (New York's electric utility) with its landmark 'campanile'; to the right is the Zeckendorf Towers apartment building, with its four pyramid-capped towers overlooking Union Square.

60 *During the summer months, numerous sailing craft dot the waters of New York Bay surrounding Ellis Island and the Statue of Liberty.*

61 *The Statue of Liberty is seen at its inspiring and dramatic best against the backdrop of Lower Manhattan.*

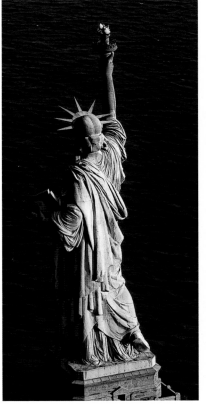

62 *The Statue of Liberty, which soars 305 ft., was dedicated in 1886. For many visitors, the inspiring statue and its park are "must see" attractions.*

63 *Strength, serenity, and timelessness mark the classic features of the symbol of Liberty.*

MID-MANHATTAN

Mid-Manhattan – from river to river, 23rd St. to 59th St., where Central Park begins. An almost perfect grid. But uniformity doesn't mean dullness. Mid-Manhattan is home to ethnic neighborhoods ranging from Brazilian through Indian to Korean; add in shopping that offers a Diamond District, a wholesale flower market, spice bazaars, and vertical malls in retrofitted department stores, include Macy's, highlight a number of world-famous skyscrapers and magnificent public buildings, throw in a number of handsome parks – and some sense of what Mid-Manhattan offers may emerge.

Take 23rd St. at Fifth Avenue, where Broadway crosses from the east to the west side of Manhattan. Directly ahead, flanking Fifth Avenue on the east side is the verdant oasis of newly refurbished Madison Square Park, its eastern margin is flanked by the elegant Neo-Classical building housing NY State Supreme Court's Appellate Division, in turn overshadowed by the tower of New York Life Insurance Co., in turn dwarfed by the massive bulk of the Metropolitan Life Insurance Co. building.

Straight ahead on the west side of Fifth Avenue at 34th street, the unmistakable Empire State Building (1931) soars skyward. Walking up to 34th St., Broadway takes one through a heady concentration of Korean import stores awash with electronic and photographic equipment, housewares, and fashion accessories. Farther east, Lexington Avenue offers a journey through the Indian spices and foodstuffs area, with restaurants beckoning.

Macy's, at Herald Sq. (34th and Broadway), anchors the retail shopping area. To the west at Seventh Avenue is Madison Square Garden, a squat silo housing convention and sports facilities that in 1963 replaced the majestic Penn Station, whose unrivalled inner halls were based on the Baths of Caracalla. The slender One Penn Plaza tower rises alongside, while the colonnaded Neo-Classical façade of the General Post Office forms a backdrop, occupying the entire 32nd to 33rd St. block.

Trade fairs and conventions are big business in New York,and the vast Jacob Javits Convention Center, a series of glass pavilions already occupying 34th to 37th Sts. off Eleventh Avenue, is slated for further expansion.

Famed 42nd St. is Mid-Manhattan's main cross-town artery. The view of the general area from a plane would include the *USS Intrepid*, an aircraft carrier that is now an Air-Sea Museum, with aircraft on its deck On West 42nd rises a unique green glass Art Deco skyscraper that once

housed McGraw-Hill; close by the immense, efficient Port Authority Terminal buildings, sprouting a web of ramps that descend into the tunnel that daily serves thousand of commuters from New Jersey and beyond.

As a vantage point from which to see New York both conserve and reinvent itself, 42nd St. and Seventh Avenue is the perfect place, and dusk is the perfect time. To the south there will be dwindling number of garment district workers pushing dress racks along the sidewalks. But to the east, along 42nd St. are the hypermodern billboard-bearing steel-and-glass towers of the 42nd St.-Times Square revival project: visual excitement, movement and light are the keywords, and the surging crowds spilling off the sidewalks show these aims have been realized.

Looking north up the broad sweep of Seventh Avenue/Broadway toward 52nd St. is a wonderland of blazing, colored light stemming from advertising panels that occupy entire building façades, their messages emphasized by ever-changing scenes drawn in brilliant neon hues. Below are lit-up movie house, hotel and theater marquees.

A block east, Sixth Avenue northbound presents itself as a canyon flanked by office towers in the steel-and-glass International Style, each sitting on a plaza; many of the plazas feature sunken concourses with some featuring a massive piece of modern art. By day the clean lines of buildings and the flows of office workers dominate the scene, but at night, the canyon is ablaze with the light streaming from a million windows.

Toward Fifth Avenue Bryant Park is a needed oasis of trees, lawns and seating, with an elegant café making it a favorite lunch place. It is also the site of annual fashion shows, for which the rear façade of the New York Public Library's palazzo-style building, a magnificent palace of learning, opened in 1911, forms a classical backdrop.

The Library's main front is on Fifth Avenue: here the broad steps and twin sculpted lions provide a meeting place for thousands daily while within is the spectacular Main Reading Room and below are elegant rooms housing special collections serving more arcane scholarship.

To the east on 42nd St. is the magnificent Beaux-Art triumph of Grand Central; Terminal (1913), where a handsome restoration of the great central hall and the shopping and dining facilities draw thousands of non-travelers. A succession of distinctive and absolutely different structures line the street going east. First the black glass box-like masses of the Marriott Hotel, then the Art Deco shaft of the iconic Chrysler Building, with its unmis-

64-65 from left to right Midtown view; the UN; the Chrysler Building spire; dusk, with the MetLife Building in the foreground.

67 For many New Yorkers the Chrysler Building remains their favorite architectural icon.

takable cascade of shimmering crescents below its spire, then, with its tree-studded atrium, the Ford Foundation Building, then Gothic-trim Tudor City.

The United Nations complex, with its Library, Secretariat Building and General Assembly Building, are of course instantly recognizable; the stark simplicity of the Secretariat contrasting with the longer, more sinuous lines of the other two low-rise structures. The campus and attached park (extending to 48th St.) make this a delightful oasis. The free-standing pierced-monolith sculpture in the forecourt of the Secretariat Building is by Barbara Hepworth, a British sculptor.

If Mid-Manhattan has a single central point it is surely Rockefeller Center. The placement of buildings, their unity of design and striking verticals that lighten the masonry cladding, with the GE Building, the tallest in the center, surrounded by ones of lesser height, of which the lowest have roof gardens, makes for a noble complex of timeless appeal. The Mall leading from Fifth Avenue to the central Concourse is a unique feature: plantings change with the seasons and at Christmas achieve high art.

Across the avenue, St. Patrick's Cathedral, designed in the high Gothic style and possessing perfect symmetry, offers a fine contrast between God and Mammon. Both St. Patrick's and Rockefeller Center seen from street level are very impressive; when seen from the air they create indelible impressions of solidity and of lightness respectively. But the traditional Fifth Avenue is visibly changing. New high rises shoehorned in on often quite small sites are thrusting high above the roof lines of their neighbors. Still farther east, on Park Avenue north of Grand Central Terminal, is another canyon of immense office towers. Straddling the avenue is the Met Life Building, whose sheer light- and breeze-blocking bulk is its main characteristic. Modern office towers line both sides of Park Avenue. At dusk, the canyon is filled with white light streaming into the growing darkness; the lack of retail establishments means a lack of colored neon.

But Park Avenue is not only office towers in the 40s and 50s giving way to grand old apartment houses farther north. There's fashionable St. Bartholomew's Church, Byzantine in style and built in brick and stone, and then the great stone pile of the Waldorf-Astoria Hotel at 47th St., temporary New York home to thousands of the world's makers and shakers. Lever House and the Seagram Building, both famous as architectural style-setters, stand nearby. Overall the East 50s is a glamorous area. Madison Avenue is already offering high-class boutiques

and specialty galleries; Lexington, and Third, Second, and First avenues are a mix of brand-new high-rise apartment towers, older 8- to 12-story buildings and century-old 6-story tenements. Every sidestreet has its small restaurants, corner groceries, and old-fashioned laundries.

The West Side is more given to business; residential blocks are farther from the center. On 47th St. diamond dealers cluster; farther west there is an amazing concentration of restaurants serving Broadway and Times Square theater patrons; at 42nd and Eighth Avenue is a high-rise development largely housing people in the theater and the arts. Much of the waterfront is still commercial; not shipping but other businesses.

Almost the northern boundary of Mid-Manhattan, 57th St. has a special character. A landmark Philip Johnson building with an iconic "broken pediment" stands at Madison Avenue. The central blocks still house many long-established art galleries, but the jewel of this broad thoroughfare is Carnegie Hall, New York's best-loved concert hall, known for its fine acoustics that yield a golden tone. It opened in 1859, with Piotr Tchaikowsky conducting the inaugural concert.

Just north, 59th St. is indeed a frontier. At Fifth Avenue, the Plaza Hotel with its green copper roof pierced by mansard windows and set off by corner turrets, stands across from Grand Army Plaza. Across the avenue rises the white-marble clad tower until recently known as the GM Building. But the true glory of 59th St. is Central Park South, extending from Fifth Avenue to Eighth Avenue and opening onto the glories of the park. Columbus Circle (the junction of Eighth Avenue and Central Park South) is now one of New York's finest architectural ensembles. Standing across from the corner of the park is the Time-Warner Building, with twin shimmering curved glass façades flanking a "Window on the Park," planned as a show-case auditorium for jazz events. The huge building is home to world-class high-fashion stores, renowned restaurants and apartments that cost several million dollars.

If Columbus Circle is the focal point of the new and stylish, then the eastern section of 59th St. (together with neighboring blocks) is much-appreciated for its charming townhouses and a quiet, neighborhood air. Just beyond Second Avenue the ramps leading to the Queensboro Bridge begin their ascent. Alongside the cantilevered steel-lattice structure built in 1909 runs a Swiss-style gondola serving residents of Roosevelt Island, a planned community in the middle of the East River.

68 Flatiron Building, erected in 1902 and now named for its shape, stands at 23rd Street, where Broadway (left) crosses Fifth Avenue.

70-71 An observer looking northeast from the block-sized Port Authority Building on Eighth Avenue and 16th Street (lower right) would see the Empire State Building soaring up at Fifth Avenue and 34th St., with midtown office towers to its north. The East River can be glimpsed toward the top of the photo.

71 top left The East River Drive is flanked by some of Manhattan's most expensive apartment houses.

71 top right Fifth Avenue begins in the exact center of this image and runs north past the Empire State Building.

72-73 Washington Square is here depicted with its famous arch; to the right is the beginning of Fifth Avenue, which divides Manhattan's West Side (left) from the East Side (right).

74 left Many older
Mid-Manhattan
office towers, like
the New York Life
Insurance Building
are enhanced by
pyramidal roofs.

74 right and 75
The Metropolitan
Life Insurance
Company's
'campanile' (1906)
and quasi-
polygonal North
Building (1931) on
Madison Avenue
and 23rd St.
overlook Madison
Square Park. The
landmark
campanile manages
to combine
Italianate and

eclectic
architectural
features, reflecting
the architectural
confidence of the
early 20th century.

76-77 The white
ribbon of Fifth
Avenue begins at
Washington Square
Park, immediately
north of the famous
arch.

78-79 East Mid-
Manhattan,
looking north with
Fifth Avenue on the
left. The
Queensboro Bridge
passes over
Roosevelt Island en
route to Queens.

80 and 81 The
Empire State
Building remains
an unchallenged
icon; it has no
near neighbors of
similar height. Its
86th-floor
Observation Deck
remains a 'must-
go' for New York's
tourist tide. The
architectural
detailing is very
restrained
compared to that
of the flamboyant
Chrysler Building,
completed a year
earlier.

82 This railcar parking yard west of Penn Station and Madison Square Garden is under consideration as the site for a proposed Olympic stadium.

83 The circular Madison Square Garden arena presents a low-rise contrast to the green roofed General Post Office to the right. Below the Garden is Penn Station, serving Long Island.

84-85 *The* USS
Intrepid, *anchored
in the Hudson River
against a backdrop
of Mid-Manhattan
highrises, is both a
popular 'Sea-Air-
Space Museum' and
an interesting
setting for social
functions.*

*86 top Strong
vertical lines
increase the
Chrysler Building's
upward thrust but
the structure has a
substantial cross-
section.*

*86 bottom and 87
Few if any
Manhattan
structures can rival
the Chrysler
Building for the
exuberant
confidence of its
decorative motifs.*

*88-89 The Met
Life Building's
uninspired bulk
(left) dwarfs Grand
Central at its base
and the elegant
Chrysler Building.
As a queen among*
*skyscrapers, the
Chrysler Building is
known for the
silvery facing of its
cascading spire. To
the right is the UN;
to its north is
Roosevelt Island.*

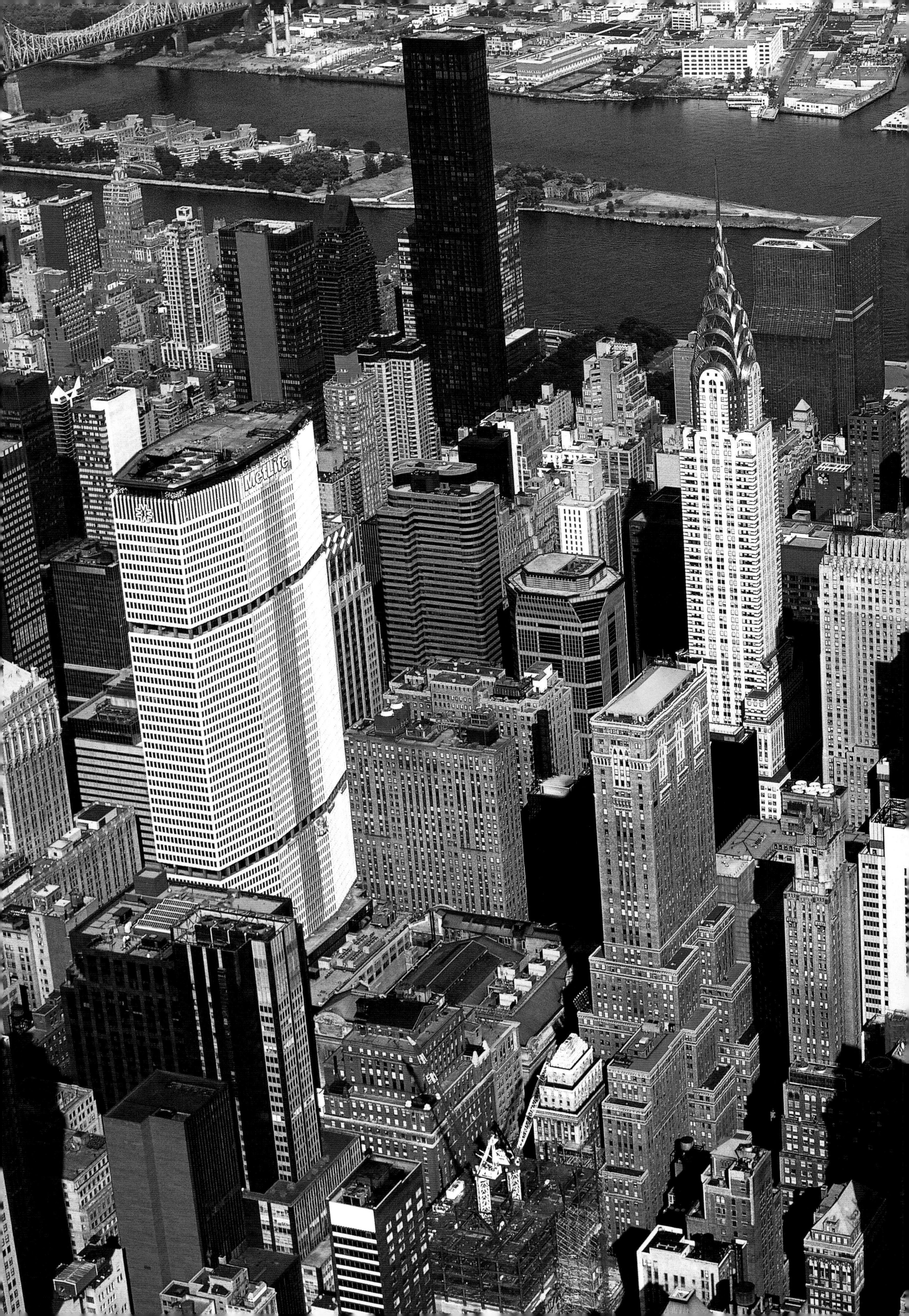
MetLife

90 The balance of forms – high-rise Secretariat, the tapered General Assembly Building, and slope-roofed Library in an open setting – give the United Nations a unique visual presence.

91 Dome, crescent and straight lines combine harmoniously in the UN's architectural design. The UN's East River frontage and adjoining park make it a tranquil haven in busy Mid-Manhattan.

92-93 Mid-Manhattan is has a huge variety of highrises. Here the pierced pediment of the AT&T Building (extreme left); the slope-roofed Citicorp Center Building, and the spire-capped Chrysler Building (center) represent distinctly different styles.

94 Visible in the upper left, the lights of Times Square, the area where Broadway and Seventh Avenue meet.

95 left The forbidding bulk of the Met Life Building casts shadows over its elegant neighbors

95 right World Plaza Building 50th Street and Eighth Avenue marks a return to an earlier architectural idiom that favored masonry cladding.

96-97 In a forest of highrises, the Citicorp Center on Lexington Avenue presents an unusual roof line. In the background is Roosevelt Island and the Queensboro Bridge.

98 A Rockefeller
Center rooftop
garden is here
viewed through the
twin spires of St.
Patrick's Cathedral.

99 The image
shows the perfect
symmetry of St.
Patrick's Cathedral,
with the towers of
Rockefeller Center
rising across Fifth
Avenue.

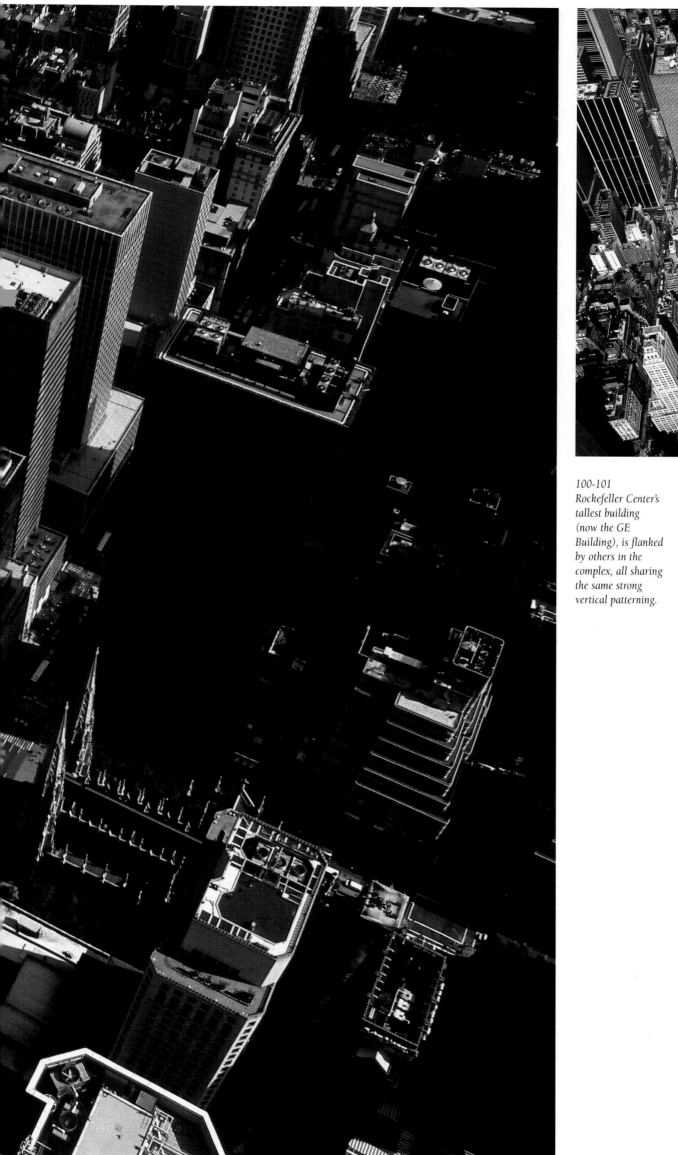

100-101
Rockefeller Center's
tallest building
(now the GE
Building), is flanked
by others in the
complex, all sharing
the same strong
vertical patterning.

101 Contemporary
steel and glass
office towers now
flank historic
Rockefeller Center,
with its solid
masonry.

102 top left and 103 top The Citicorp Center's sloping roof contrasts with the turrets and flat-tops of older buildings. The roof is not an architectural whimsy but a massive solar energy panel.

102 top right The exuberant copper pyramid and cupola of the New York Central Building is a Midtown icon.

102-103 The Plaza Hotel, at Fifth Avenue and Central Park South, reflects European architectural motifs.

103 bottom This triangle is no a work of art but the site of air-conditioning intakes and exhausts.

104-105 The clustered towers of central Mid-Manhattan, looking northwest toward Central Park, flanked by Central Park West and its

luxury apartment houses. The "broken pediment" building with the solar panel is the AT&T Building at Madison Avenue and 57th Street.

106 and 107 bottom right A cone of brilliant light . . . the Chrysler Building spire at night.

107 left 4 Times Square's radio mast soars skyward; top left is the golden pyramid of the World Plaza Building at 50th St. and Eighth Avenue.

107 top right The sun goes down; the lights of Manhattan skyscrapers will soon start illuminating the night.

108-109 Looking north with the MetLife, Citicorp Center, Chrysler, General Electric, and Empire State buildings all lit up.

UPPER MANHATTAN

From the air, Central Park, flanked by the Upper East and Upper West Sides, each a mix of high-rise apartment buildings, tenements, and retail businesses, seizes the eye. Manhattan's green heart extends from 59th St. to 110th St., on land set aside in 1853, when the city's patricians decided that Manhattan should match the parks of European capitals. Fortunately, the area was too rocky for other uses.

The formidable duo of Vaux and Olmsted, the park's designers, created a masterpiece, taking advantage of topography and sinking and bridging transverse roadways, ensuring a haven for pedestrians. The park's many elements delight all strollers. Looking north, there's the Bird Sanctuary and the Sheep Meadow, a big open area that draws strollers, dog-walkers and child exercisers. Just east is the small Zoo, beloved by local children.. Then there's the great tree-lined Mall ending in a magnificent balustraded terrace overlooking the Bethesda Fountain. Beyond is the Boating Lake, and then almost at the park's center is the Great Lawn, a venue for concerts, overlooked by Belvedere Castle, whose turret provides splendid views of the Delacorte Theater, the Shakespeare Garden and the farther reaches of the park.

North of the Lawn is the huge Jacqueline Kennedy Onassis Reservoir; fitness enthusiasts run around it at dawn and dusk. Toward the park's northern boundary are tennis courts, the elegant Conservatory Gardens, the Meer, the Lasker Pool and Skating Rink, as well as numerous tree-shaded walks and, for the energetic, the Ravine and the Great Hill. Some twenty or so architecturally impressive gates, each celebrating a profession or group, adorn the park's perimeter.

Fifth Avenue forms the park's eastern boundary, one marked by staid but luxurious apartment houses. In the avenue's lower reach, Temple El-Emmanuel, with a typical arched cross-section, breaks the line of residential buildings. The Frick Collection, at 70th St., offers Old Master paintings in the palatial home that Henry Clay Frick, a turn-of-the-century steel millionaire, bequeathed to the nation. From 80th to 84th streets (within the park) stands the massive Metropolitan Museum of Art; now both

a cultural and social venue. Farther north on Museum Mile is the white spiral of the Guggenheim Museum, considered one of Frank Lloyd Wright's masterpieces. Next door is the National Academy of Design, located in an elegant townhouse. In striking contrast to these two institutions is the huge Georgian mansion built for the steel multimillionaire Andrew Carnegie, now housing the Cooper-Hewitt Museum of Design. Also located on the prestigious of Museum Mile are the Jewish Museum, known for outstanding exhibitions, and the International Center for Photography, with its archival collections.

Body as well as soul is catered for: at 98th St. stand the strikingly modern buildings of Mt. Sinai Medical Center; just beyond, at 103rd St. is the dignified older building of New York Academy of Medicine, with its unrivaled library. Those in search of musical and choral offerings can visit St. Nicholas Russian Orthodox Cathedral at 97th St. Then, for the visitor keen to check on questions about the city, at 104th St. is the Museum of the City of New York.

Parallel to Fifth is Madison Avenue, which still retains many smaller buildings, home to many fine antiques, high fashion, and design boutiques, as well as elegant restaurants. It is also home to the Whitney Museum, which Gertrude Vanderbilt Whitney, a sculptor, founded in 1930, after the Metropolitan Museum highhandedly refused her gift of work by living American painters. The museum's current home at 74th St, designed by Marcel Breuer, is a dark brick building that widens as it rises. The Whitney Biennal is a recognized showcase for new American art. Another iconic Upper East Side building is the vast Seventh Regiment Armory; here annual antiques shows and equally prestigious antiquarian book fairs draw thousands of enthusiasts.

The buildings on Park, Lexington, Third, Second and First avenues and their cross streets are home to an innumerable army of New Yorkers determined to live on the "fashionable Upper East Side." Most pay excessively high rents for the privilege - and neighborhood stores, often offering expensive imported food delicacies and glamorous apparel, tempt tastes but burden credit cards. In every way, the Upper East Side is chic designer and tasteful importer territory, with never quite satisfied customers. The Hungarian community, with its tastes and preferences reflected

110-111 from left to right Upper West Side; the Guggenheim Museum; the Century Apartments; the Time-Warner Building.

113 The twin-towered San Remo apartment house offers magnificent views over Central Park. It was

completed just before the Great Depression, and is one of the architect Emery Roth's many luxury buildings.

in shops on the streets just below 86th St, and the German community of Yorkville centered on 86th St. are only a very faint shadow of what they were a half century ago; restauranteurs and storeowners die and their cuisines and businesses die with them.

Beyond First Avenue lie the short stretches of York and East End avenues; they occupy land edging toward the East River. Just beyond East End Avenue, on a bluff at 89th St., is Gracie Mansion in its delightful small park. Built for Archibald Gracie in 1799, it is now the official residence of the Mayor of the City of New York.

The Upper West Side is a narrower swathe of territory than the Upper East Side, but Riverside Park, with the Hudson beyond, gives everyone easy access to exercise and open-air leisure. The area prides itself on its distinctive differences from the somewhat conservative Upper East Side, its urban "neighbor" across the park. Many residents consider the Upper West Side to be more liberal, with more street life and more varied retail businesses; others note the contribution of Jewish residents with their vitality and love of theater and music.

Central Park West in every way matches Fifth Avenue for handsome apartment houses; in fact, many are more architecturally distinctive than those that face them on the Fifth Avenue side. Breaking the skyline are the exuberant twin towers of the Century, the Majestic, the San Remo, and the Eldorado; the Dakota (when built in 1884 it was "in the wilds"), the turreted Beresford, and other palatial buildings are equally prestigious places to live. On Broadway, imagination plays a larger role: for sheer exuberance of detailing the Ansonia at 71st St. and the nearby Dorilton and a dozen other buildings are unrivaled.

The Upper West Side prides itself on its cultural resources, and the severe Classical building of the New-York Historical Society is a solid presence on Central Park West. Farther north at 81st St. is the American Museum of Natural History, a treasure house of magnificent displays and dioramas of wild life that is also famous for its mineral and gem collections. Its new glass-cube addition containing the silver-sphere Planetarium contrasts sharply with limestone and red-tile of the main building.

A brand-new building at 59th St. and Central Park West is already a hub of activity. Two broad towers with curved glass façades overlook the southwest cor-

ner of Central Park; between them is a concert hall high above the park, in which jazz will be the main fare. Just north, on Columbus Avenue, is Lincoln Center for the Performing Arts. New York State Theater, The Metropolitan Opera and Avery Fisher Hall flank the central plaza, while other performance halls and the Juilliard School of Music fill out the complex.

Behind Lincoln Center, West End Avenue runs north. Like Park Avenue, it is flanked by huge old apartment houses. By comparison, Riverside Drive is much more varied; with smaller buildings which offer many architectural delights. Not to be missed is the long-established "floating village" of the West 79th St. Boat Basin, where the hardy live year-round on their water-borne homes.

Upper West Siders enjoy life. The area abounds with ethnic restaurants: Chinese, Vietnamese, Thai, Indonesian, Greek, Cuban, Latin-American of every style. Ask for any exotic cuisine and someone can point out where it is to be had. Theater and music flourish in off-beat venues. Small cafes punctuate many of the side streets, where handsome old brownstones house a burgeoning population of the young and the hopeful. A large number seem to be film-makers, actors, writer, or dancers. They are making their way in New York: what more can they ask for?

Farther north, at 110th St. in Harlem, the massive Triborough Bridge passes over the stadiums, tennis courts, and pool of conjoined Randall and Ward's Island, with its web of elevated highways linking Manhattan, Queens and the Bronx. Still farther north, adjoining Broadway from 114th to 121st Streets is Columbia University's immense urban campus. Seen from above, the intricate geometry of the quadrangle and courtyards and the green copper-roofed buildings, with the circular Low Memorial Library at the center, is truly impressive. Heading north and passing over Harlem's Morningside and Marcus Garvey parks one would look down on a much narrower Manhattan, an urban spine flanked by parks and riverfronts. On the west, the lengthy span of the George Washington Bridge (1931) links Upper Manhattan to New Jersey.

The last sight is the most atypical: close to Manhattan's hilly, wooded northern tip is rugged Fort Tryon Park. In it stands the Cloisters, a gem of a hilltop monastery-museum, one which the New World assembled from religious structures salvaged from the Old World.

114 Columbia University's impressive campus on the Upper West Side extends over eight full blocks from 112th to 120th Streets. The three domed buildings are top, Butler Library; center, Low Memorial Library; and foreground, St. Paul's Chapel.

*116 top and 117 top
The century
Apartments at 62nd
St. and Central Park
West is characterized
by twin towers.*

*116-117 The twin
tower-tops of the
Time-Warner
Building at
Columbus Circle
(59th St. and*

*Eighth Avenue)
support air-
conditioning
equipment. Central
Park can be seen in
the upper corner.*

*117 bottom The
buildings flanking or
close to Central Park
present an amazing
variety of
architectural detail.*

118 top Baseball in the park or strolls along the Hudson: the Upper West Side offers both.

118 bottom Central Park West is one of New York's finest residential avenues, and the Hudson is within easy reach.

118-119 The soaring twin towers of the new Time-Warner Building cast their shadow over Central Park's southwest corner.

119 top The Fifth Avenue Synagogue forms a contrast to the high-rise apartment houses that look onto the park.

120-121 This spectacular image looks down Central Park from 110th to 59th Street, with the circular Lasker Pool and Rink and the Jacqueline Kennedy Onassis Reservoir clearly visible. Fifth Avenue is on the left, Central Park West on the right.

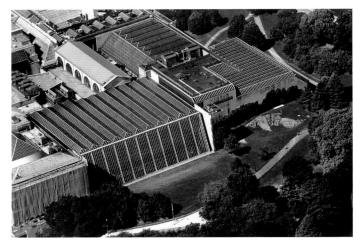

122 top The Metropolitan Museum built a new wing to house the Temple of Dendur, acquired when the Aswan Dam was constructed on the Nile.

122-123 In this image are shown the Metropolitan Museum's Fifth Avenue façade and steps; the pediments above the paired columns have yet to be sculpted.

123 top and 124-125 The Metropolitan Museum, one of the world's great treasure houses of art, flanks Fifth Avenue, extending well into Central Park.

123 bottom This elegant addition to the Metropolitan Museum houses the distinguished Lehman Collection.

126-177 This panoramic view shows the West Side Highway running north from a new housing area and entering tree-clad Riverside Park at 72nd Street. The West Side Highway is flanked by handsome older apartment houses, which are prestige addresses.

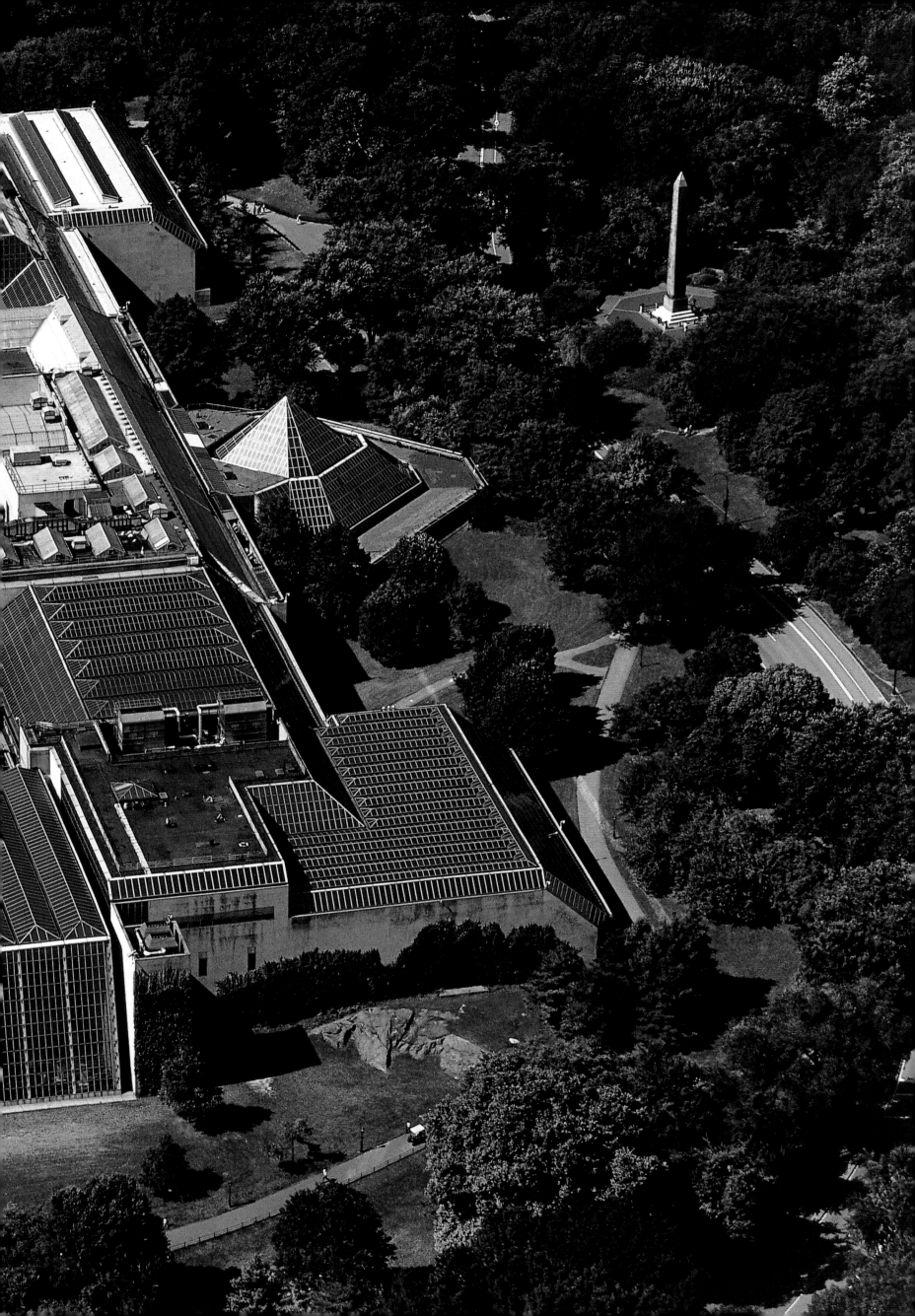

128 top and 128-129 The Guggenheim Museum, the Church of the Heavenly Rest, and the Andrew Carnegie residence (now the Cooper-Hewitt Museum) contrast dramatically with their apartment house neighbors.

129 top The famed Museum of Natural History is a Central Park West landmark and a top-tier attraction for New Yorkers and visitors.

129 bottom The height of most Central Park West apartment houses blocks the view for those living in rear.

130-131 This image looking east, shows the twin towers of the San Remo and the Majestic apartment houses overlook Central Park.

132-133 Looking east from Fifth Avenue, the borough of Queens is visible beyond the three red-banded smokestacks.

134 Churches flourish in Harlem, drawing large congregations. Many serve as neighborhood anchors and provide needed community services.

135 A view north from mid-Harlem with the George Washington Bridge on the upper left.

136-137 The interdenominational Riverside Church, on Riverside Drive and 122nd St., was built in the 1930s with funding contributed by John D. Rockefeller, Jr. It is famous for its carillon and as a liberal forum.

THE OUTER

BOROUGHS

The boroughs have rich histories, impressive architecture, universities, cultural centers, and diverse ethnic communities forming a rich h mosaic. Many of New York's cultural and hishistoric jewels are in the boroughs, together with many of the finest parks and beaches. Each borough contributes vitally to New York's unrivaled attractions.

From the air, the Harlem River stands out, separating the Bronx from Upper Manhattan. The Bronx is indeed "a borough of parks and beaches": Van Cortlandt and Pelham Bay parks are great swathes of turf, woodland, and water. Also visible is the spectacular Bronx Zoo, with over 3,500 animals, many roaming in open habitats. The adjacent New York Botanical Garden is also world class; spectacular hothouses, groves, and climatic zones accommodate an unrivaled wealth of flora.

In the northern Bronx, Fieldston's winding streets adjoining Van Cortlandt Park, and hilly, wooded Riverdale, with its park overlooking the Hudson, will be visible. In the northeastern Bronx, in total contrast, stands a massive monument to mid-1960s Modernism, the 35 huge apartment towers of Co-Op City, containing some 15,000 apartments. Not far distant in Long Island Sound is City Island, a haven of small homes and boat-yards.

The scene changes in the southeastern Bronx; waterfront communities abound. Throg's Neck, fronting onto Eastchester Bay and the East River, is one such community; nearby the soaring Throg's Neck and Whitestone bridges link the Bronx to Queens. Fort Schuyler (now part of New York State Maritime College) faces Fort Totten on the Queens side; both were part of New York's waterway defenses.

Standing proud in the mid-Bronx is the towering new glass-clad County Courthouse, almost adjoining are Fordham University and Bronx Park, through which the Bronx River flows. Atop University Heights is the Hall of Fame for Great Americans, a huge colonnade housing bronze busts that encircles three Neo-Classical buildings, now part of City College.

Though the South Bronx suffered a massive decline in the 1960s, rows of attractive new two-family homes and gardens witness the area's economic rebirth, attracting new immigrants and adding to the quality of life. The Grand Concourse, with its Art Deco apartment houses, is also regaining its former luster. For local baseball fans, Yankee Stadium, once home to the Bronx Bombers and now to the New York Yankees, remains a nearby mecca. Other sports thrive: Van Cortlandt Park hosts rugby (British and Irish), cricket (West Indians and British), hurling (the Irish) and tennis and golf. There is indeed something for everyone: hence the weekend crowds.

From overhead, Brooklyn appears endless, but distinctive features abound. Most dramatic is Prospect Park with its lake, Long Meadow, wooded Ravine, and Concert Grove among other "rustic" attractions. Grand Army Plaza, with a backdrop of handsome apartment houses, provides a fitting entrance to the park, while in easy reach on Eastern Parkway are the modern Brooklyn Public Library and the Classical-style Brooklyn Museum, with its dramatic glass-roofed entry plaza. Once culturally satisfied, visitors can stroll in the attractively planted Botanic Garden. The much smaller Fort Greene Park boasts a distinctive feature: the columnar Prison Ship Martyrs' Monument, honoring some 12,000 American who died below decks on British ships during the Revolutionary War.

Brooklyn has a highly varied series of waterfronts. Above those facing Manhattan are the approaches to the Brooklyn, Manhattan, and Williamsburg bridges. All three are highly photogenic; from-the-air photographs capture them in every sort of light. Brooklyn's most spectacular span is the Verrazano-Narrows Bridge, soaring over the water from Bay Ridge to Staten Island, a undisputed triumph of vision and engineering.

From above, the south and southeastern Brooklyn waterfronts are spectacular. Coney Island (not an island at all!) and Brighton Beach offer huge expanses of sand; in summer thousands of Manhattanites flock there to join the local population. Noticeable from afar are the clusters of new high-rise apartment communities. Looking down to the east, Gateway National Recreation Area swings into view, where extensive parkland runs down to Jamaica Bay, rich in protected wildlife. From the air, Gateway National Recreation Area presents itself as a huge bay, dotted with still wild islands, large and small, across which runs the silver thread of the rail line going out to Rockaway Peninsula, passing a modest on-the-water community of turn-of-the-century houses on stilts. The Bay's sheer size and "a different world" quality remain a constant surprise

138-139 from left to right Jamaica Bay; two views of the Verrazano-Narrows Bridge; Yankee Stadium in the Bronx.

141 The mighty Verrazano-Narrows Bridge, New York's longest span, crosses Lower New York Bay to link Brooklyn and Staten Island.

Arts and education are well served: for eager audiences, the much-loved Brooklyn Academy of Music's three auditoria present often avant-garde music, drama, and dance; and in academia, Brooklyn College, housed in 1930s Neo-Georgian buildings, is held in high respect. Brooklyn is a proud borough - with reason.

Historically, Queens has been known for quiet homes on quiet streets. People flying into either LaGuardia or JFK airports will note whole neighborhoods of private homes and small apartment houses, occasional institutional complexes on landscaped plazas, parkland, and a lot of shoreline. But airports need support services, and industrial facilities are also visible.

Those really wanting to live "at the shore" are well served. From Far Rockaway to Breezy Point, homes look out over the Atlantic; inland lies Jamaica Bay, incorporating Gateway National Recreation Area. In some areas homes have built on pilings, directly over the water, looking like New England fishing-village homes. Jacob Riis Park, named for the great 19th-century crusader against slums, runs from ocean to bay. The park and its boardwalk are favorites among Rockaway residents. At Rockaway's eastern end is Breezy Point, a gated private beach community.

Queens has large and still-growing immigrant communities. Asians are a vibrant presence in Flushing and adjoining areas; temples, clothing stores, and specialty foods are common. In Jackson Heights the note is predominantly Indian, and sari and jewelry stores abound. Other areas have large Latin-American populations, adding another range of restaurants, foodstuffs, and music.

Queens residents are well served by a necklace of parks. Flushing Meadow-Corona Park and nearby Kissena, Cunningham, and Alley parks form a near-continuous greensward, each park offering splendid vistas and walks. Kissena Park is home to Queens Botanical Garden, which houses a fine arboretum. Flushing Meadows-Corona Park, site of the 1964 World's Fair, is graced by a number of striking avant-garde buildings commissioned for the occasion and retained after it ended. They include the Unisphere and the elevated Terrace on the Park, as well as the New York Pavilion, which became the Queens Museum (it has a huge model of New York City), and the imaginative Hall of Science. Queens in also home to the taste-setting P.S. 1 Contemporary Art Center.

Sports are well served in Queens. Shea Stadium, home of the New York Mets, draws tens of thousands of home-team enthusiasts. The borough has long been home to international tennis tournaments; in the past they took place in Forest Hills but now use larger, more modern facilities in Flushing Meadows.

From overhead, Staten Island seems huge, a patchwork quilt of small townships and modest clusters of houses and gardens. Only St. George, with the Ferry Terminal, Borough Hall, and the Island's administrative buildings, looks like a traditional town.

Among the boroughs only Staten Island has real wooded hills. Exclusive Todt Hill is dotted with expensive homes and occasional big mansions. Dongan Hills presents two surprises, Staten Island Lighthouse (well inland and 230 ft high), and the Jacques Marchais Museum of Tibetan Art, housed in a Tibetan-style monastery on a wooded hillside, with descending terraced gardens.

From overhead, Sailors' Snug Harbor, Staten Island's finest architectural complex, is unmistakable. Situated in an 83-acre park of stately trees close to St. George and the Kill van Kull (the waterway separating Staten Island and New Jersey), this haven for "aged and decrepit" mariners was built in the 1830s on a now unimaginable scale. Five enormous Greek-temple style structures face a second row of similar structures across a broad mall. These buildings housed the retired sailors, who had a concert hall, library, church and every other needed facility. Snug Harbor and its well-tended park is now a cultural center, with the buildings sensitively restored for contemporary uses.

Staten Island's many other attractions include High Rock Conservation Area, a 94-acre forest and wild life refuge. Overall, creek-side parks and numerous patches of woodland help give the borough a still often bucolic, occasionally rugged look. Another surprise that Staten Island presents is a whole "village" of historic buildings, the Richmontown Restoration, were some 30 restored buildings, many with furniture, provide a dramatic sense of life in the past. They are survivors of the modest mid-island township that served as the Island's administrative center from the 1750s until the 1850s.

Development came late to Staten Island, and historic survivals are numerous. At the island's southern tip is the Conference House (ca. 1670), a fieldstone manor where George Washington met with the British. Of much later vintage is Austen House in Rosebank, an exquisite Victorian cottage where the pioneer photographer Alice Austen lived. Beautifully sited at the Narrows, the entrance to New York Bay, house and garden are a delight.

143 Yankee Stadium is situated in the Bronx, "the borough of parks, universities, and waterfronts," whose numerous attractive residential neighborhoods are home to many thousands who work in Manhattan.

144 top Parked yellow school buses are a familiar sight in New York's four outer boroughs. Shown here is a bus park in the Bronx.

144-145 In this image is a partly "wrapped" George Washington Bridge. The Little Red Lighthouse on the Manhattan side of the Hudson is a storied icon.

145 top The High Bridge Watch Tower was once part of the Croton Aqueduct system that brought water through the Bronx to Manhattan. The tower (actually on the Manhattan side of the Harlem River) now overlooks a swimming pool.

145 center More than a dozen bridges span the Harlem River, linking the Bronx to Manhattan.

145 bottom The Bronx has many fine older collegiate and institutional buildings, as shown here. A generally Georgian style with Classical notes was very popular in the late 19th and early 20th centuries.

146 top and 146-147 Showcase stadiums and immaculate patterned turf (usually artificial) are all part of the mystique of contemporary baseball.

147 On game nights, Yankee Stadium, just across the Harlem River from Upper Manhattan, draws thousands of eager New York Yankee fans.

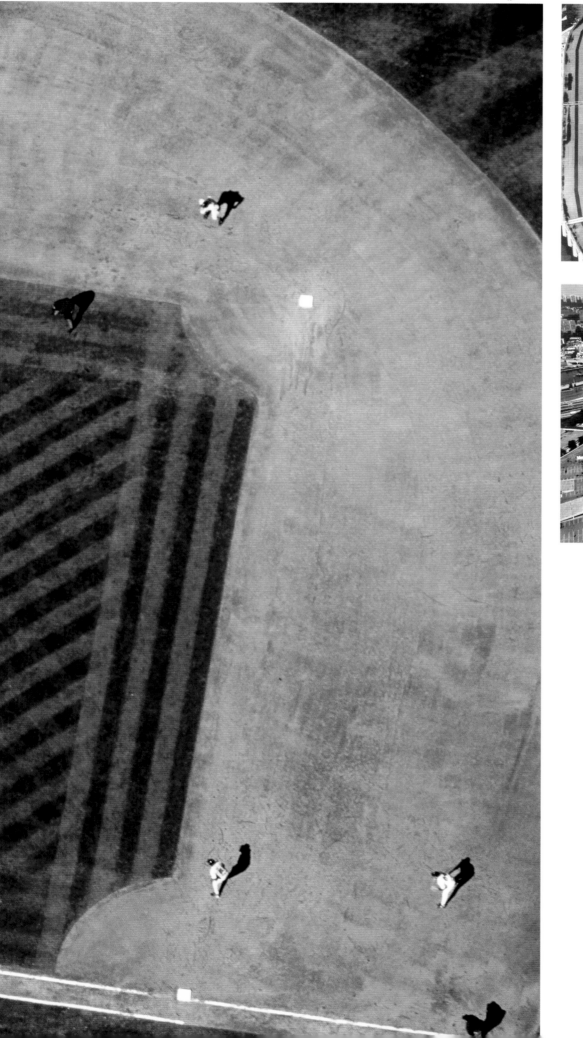

*148 top Bronx
Park includes a
fine piazza and
garden forum.*

*148-149 The
Bronx Botanical
Gardens'
Conservatory*

*Range houses world-
famous plant
collections. The
extensive Gardens
share Bronx Park
with the equally
famous Bronx Zoo,
a pace-setter in
animal care.*

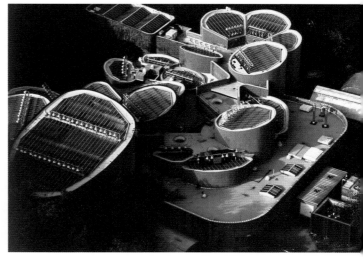

*149 top The old
Elephant House at
the Bronx Zoo is
now the Zoo
Center; the
elephants roam
freely on the open
range.*

*149 bottom The
Bird House, one of
the Bronx Zoo's
finest attractions,
is an ultra-modern
series of buildings.*

150 top The Verrazano-Narrows Bridge is heavily used by vehicles carrying freight landed in the Brooklyn and Staten Island maritime terminals. Manhattan is no longer a major cargo entry point.

150-151 The Staten Island approaches to the Verrazano-Narrows Bridge. The park is federal land; historic Ft. Wadsworth, guarding the Narrows, can be seen to the left, on the bay.

151 top Spanning the Narrows, the Verrazano Bridge marks the divide between the Upper Bay (north, to the left) and the Lower Bay, opening onto the Atlantic.

151 bottom The Verrazano-Narrows Bridge combines uncluttered design with unrivaled traffic capacity.

152 and 153 On Marathon Day, thousands runners turn out and the Verrazano-Narrows Bridge carries a human tide. Many but not all New York bridges have pedestrian pathways.

154-155 Here is the small community of Foxbury, close to the western end of Rockaway Peninsula. For. Tilden, a historic defense structure, is on the upper left, near the bridge ramp.

156-157 One of the many communities fronting onto Jamaica Bay. Sections of both Brooklyn and Queens face the Bay, which incorporates Gateway National Recreation Area.

157 top For homeowners on Jamaica Bay, parking a boat can be as problematic as parking a car!

157 bottom Many Jamaica Bay homeowners see a private dock as a necessary addition to their homes.

158-159 Handsome older warehouse and commercial buildings, now being renovated, and new miniparks characterize the Brooklyn waterfront below the approaches to the Manhattan and Brooklyn bridges.

160 The Statue of Liberty dominates Manhattan Bay in the orange and warm lights of sunset.

All the pictures inside the book are by Antonio Attini/Archivio White Star except for the following:

Kevin Fleming/Corbis/Contrasto: pages 2-3
Jim Wark: pages 4-5, 8, 24, 82, 126-127
Alan Schein Photography/Corbis/Contrasto: page 9
World Sat: page 11
Hammon, Jensen, Wallen and Associates, NGS: page 12
Alamy Images: pages 60, 68, 106, 160
Jason Hawkes: pages 62 right, 63, 99
David Zimmerman/Corbis/Contrasto: pages 72-73, 104-105
Falke/laif/Contrasto: pages 135 left, 153
Timothy Fadek/Corbis Sygma/Contrasto: page 137
David Alan Harvey/Magnum Photos/Contrasto: page 140, 141, 142-143
Yann Arthus-Bertrand/Corbis/Contrasto: pages 146-147, 152

PHOTO CREDITS

The photographer would like to thank Pegasus Flight
(www.pegasus-flight.com)